THE
OLYMPCS

MATT CHRISTOPHER®

The #1 Sports Series for Kids

★ LEGENDARY SPORTS EVENTS ★

THE OLYMPICS

Unforgettable Moments of the Games

LITTLE, BROWN AND COMPANY
Books for Young Readers
New York   Boston

Little, Brown and Company

Hachette Book Group USA
237 Park Avenue, New York, NY 10017
Visit our Web site at www.lb-kids.com

www.mattchristopher.com

First Edition: July 2008

Matt Christopher® is a registered trademark of
Matt Christopher Royalties, Inc.

Text written by Stephanie Peters

ISBN-13: 978-0-316-01118-1
ISBN-10: 0-316-01118-5

10 9 8 7 6 5 4 3 2 1

COM-MO

Printed in the United States of America

Contents

THE
OLYMPICS

✶ PROLOGUE ✶

Imagine that you are posed on a gym mat in the middle of a huge stadium, waiting for the music that signals the start of your floor routine. Or perhaps you are atop a huge snow-covered slope, counting the seconds before you burst forth from the gate and slalom down the hill at breakneck speed. Or maybe you are crouched on the track, feet pressed against the starting blocks, hands steadying you in the final moments before the starting gun sets you free.

The eyes of thousands of spectators are on you. Television cameras from nations around the world train their lenses on you. Your heart is thumping. Adrenaline courses through you. Your body is a finely tuned machine, the epitome of fitness and the result of months, even years of training. Your mind is focused on one thing, and one thing only: giving the athletic performance of your life.

You are an Olympian, and this is your moment.

But you are not alone. Chances are, many people have worked very hard to get you to this moment.

Your parents have been there from the beginning. They saw something special in you — and helped you see it, too. They drove you to practices, meets, games, and competitions. They paid for your equipment, uniforms, classes, and training. They cheered the loudest when you succeeded, held your hand when you failed, urged you to be the best you could be.

Your teachers, coaches, trainers — all lent their knowledge and skills to help you hone the talent you were born with and lift you to ever greater heights. They prepared you for this, the most challenging moment of your life.

Your siblings and friends made sure you "kept it real." Even as you reached for the stars, they joked with you, played with you, and fought with you. They know you not just as a superior athlete, but as a person. No matter how you fare, they will be there for you.

But in the end, you are the one who got you to this moment. And as you ready yourself for the most important athletic contest of your life, you join the ranks of thousands of others who have taken part in the most honored and longest-lived sporting tradition in history: the Olympic Games.

★ CHAPTER ONE ★
776 BC–AD 1894

The Olympics Begin, End, and Begin Again

The Olympic Games were born in 776 BC in ancient Greece. Back then, Greece was divided into small kingdoms called city-states. These city-states were often at war with one another. Then, according to legend, the famous Oracle of Delphi told one king of a way to bring peace to the land — at least temporarily.

"Announce a race to honor Zeus, the king of the gods," the Oracle instructed him. "Open the race to all male athletes of Greece, and then declare a truce so that these athletes can travel to the contest in safety. This truce will foster peace."

Few people ever disobeyed the Oracle, and this king was no exception. He chose Olympia, a religious sanctuary dedicated to Zeus, as the location

5

for the race. The Olympic Games take their name from this site.

The first Olympics consisted of a single race called the *stade*. The *stade* was a sprint of about 600 feet and was run barefoot on a dirt track. A cook named Koroibos won the race in 776 BC, becoming the first Olympic champion.

From then on, the Olympics were held every four years. As the Games grew in popularity, new events were added that tested speed, agility, and strength. By the fifth century BC, the Games were five days long.

Like today's athletes, the ancient Greek competitors worked with trainers for many months to hone their skills and increase their physical abilities. In July of an Olympic year, they traveled to Olympia to train for one final month under the watchful eyes of the ten Olympic judges.

The competitors were all male citizens of Greece. Few women were allowed near Olympia during the games, in part because the athletes trained and competed in the nude. Slaves and non-Greeks were not permitted to compete because they were not considered worthy of the honor.

Spectators arrived in August, just before the Games were to begin, transforming the area around Olympia into a colorful fairground. On Opening Day, the crowd hurried to watch the athletes march into Olympia's stadium. Then, before a statue of Zeus and the Olympic judges, the competitors solemnly swore that they had been training for ten months of that year and that they would obey the rules of the Games. That afternoon, boys ages twelve to eighteen ran, wrestled, and boxed for top honors, giving spectators a look at Greece's future Olympians.

The next morning everyone flocked to the hippodrome, a dirt oval track about three-quarters of a mile around, for the chariot races. At the sound of the trumpet, the charioteers whipped their horses to full speed for distances of two and a half miles to eight miles. It took great skill to avoid collisions, and many races featured at least one bloody crash that wounded or even killed horses and drivers.

Next up were horse races. Jockeys rode bareback,

leaning forward to urge their steeds ever faster. The going was rough, for no one bothered to rake the dirt after the chariot races. Horses sometimes stumbled, taking their riders with them to the ground.

The afternoon was given over to the pentathlon, a five-part competition of discus, javelin, jumping, running, and wrestling.

A discus looks like a modern Frisbee — but is much larger and heavier! Some ancient discuses weighed as much as five and a half pounds. Experts disagree about whether ancient athletes whirled around before releasing the discus, as modern competitors do, or if they threw from a standing position. Either way, throwing one any distance required great strength.

The ancient javelin had a length of thong twisted about the shaft. The competitor wrapped the thong around two fingers, took a running start, and then hurled the spear overhand, releasing the thong as he did. The thin leather strap helped the javelin fly true.

After the javelin came the long jump. Historians aren't sure if a jumper got a running start or jumped from a standing position. Pictures on ancient pottery show some athletes swinging heavy hand weights while jumping — a difficult maneuver, according to modern jumpers who have tried to duplicate it.

If a single athlete won these first three events, he was declared the victor and the pentathlon ended. If not, the final two events, a *stade* sprint and a wrestling match, took place. The man who placed highest in all five events was the champion.

Three races took place on the third day: the long-distance *dolichos* (approximately two and a half to two and three-quarters miles); the *diaulos,* which was two lengths of the stadium; and the one-length *stade.* Many athletes competed in this last race, for the entire Games were named after its winner, a huge honor.

Wrestling started the fourth day, followed by boxing — no gloves in ancient times, only bare fists — and then a violent sport called the *pankration. Pankration* means all-strength, and athletes who competed in this event certainly needed every ounce of muscle they could muster. The one-on-one matches combined wrestling, martial arts, and boxing, with the goal being to force one's opponent to admit defeat. Only biting and eye gouging were against the rules.

After the *pankration* came the final competition of the Olympics, the *hoplitodromos*. This event was another footrace — with a twist. Runners wore helmets and carried heavy shields while running two stadium lengths. The Olympic judges provided identical shields so that no competitor could cheat by carrying a lighter one.

The fifth day of the Olympics celebrated the victors. Standing in the Temple of Zeus and surrounded by cheering crowds, each champion was crowned with a wreath of olive branches. Some had their achievements noted in song, poetry, and art and thus have come down to us through history.

There's Milo, a wrestler who supposedly built up his tremendous strength by carrying the same calf every day. Milo's strength grew greater as the calf grew into a bull. Milo won his first Olympic wrestling match as a boy in 540 BC, and then five times more in the next twenty years.

Leonidas, a runner from Rhodes, was one of the fastest men of his time. He won the *dolichos*, the *stade*, and the *diaulos* four Olympics in a row, becoming the most famous "tripler" in ancient history. The Olympics of 164 BC, 160 BC, 156 BC, and 152 BC are all named for him.

Arrakhion, a *pankration* athlete, made a name for himself not only because he won his event but because he died immediately after being declared the winner! In the heat of the match, Arrakhion's opponent caught him in a leg hold and beat him mercilessly. But Arrakhion didn't give up. He wrenched one of the man's toes back and broke it. The pain was so intense that the opponent conceded the match. But a moment later, Arrakhion died from the man's blows!

Then there's Diagoras of Rhodes, the boxing champion of 464 BC and father of an Olympic dynasty. His three sons, Damagetos (*pankration*), Akousilaos (boxing), and Dorieus (*pankration*), were all Olympians, as were two of his grandsons. After Damagetos and Akousilaos won in 448 BC, they carried Diagoras around the stadium on their shoulders.

The Olympics were held without fail every four

years from 776 BC to AD 393. During those centuries, the ancient world underwent drastic changes. In 146 BC, Greece lost a war with Rome. The Roman Empire absorbed much of Greece's culture and traditions, including the Olympics. They continued to hold the Games until AD 393, when the Roman emperor Theodosius took the throne. Theodosius was a Christian and he made it a priority to wipe paganism from his empire. The Olympics were very closely tied with the worship of Zeus, a pagan god, so Theodosius banned the Games. After the ban, Olympia's buildings fell into ruin and much of her history was lost.

Fifteen hundred years would pass before the tradition of the Games was brought out of obscurity. In 1894, a French baron named Pierre de Coubertin set to work to convince an international assembly to revive the ancient Games. Luckily for sports lovers the world over, he succeeded — and in the summer of 1896, the first modern Olympic Games were held.

Fittingly, Athens, Greece, was chosen as the site.

☆ CHAPTER TWO ☆

1896–1916

First Olympic Decades

"I hereby proclaim the opening of the First International Olympic Games in Athens!"

These were the words spoken by King George I of Greece on April 6, 1896. The audience of one hundred thousand people cheered, a flock of pigeons was released into the air, and a 150-member chorus sang the new Olympic Anthem.

The Olympic Games were back.

James B. Connolly, a 27-year-old athlete from the United States, made history by winning the first medal in the modern Olympics. His event was the triple jump, then known as "a hop, a step, and a jump." For his victory, he was awarded a silver medal (there were no gold medals then) with Zeus's portrait on one side and the Greek Acropolis on the other. He also received a certificate and an olive branch, a tribute to the champions of the ancient Games.

The United States also brought discus thrower Robert Garrett. Garrett excelled in track and field at Princeton University, but he had never even held a discus. When Garrett learned that discus was to be an event at the Olympics, he and a Princeton professor made one based on the ancient discus. The result was a cumbersome object weighing almost thirty pounds. When Garrett couldn't throw the homemade discus any great distance, he decided not to enter the event in Athens after all.

Then he arrived at the Games — and learned that the modern discus weighed six pounds, not thirty! He entered the event and won with a throw that went a full seven and a half inches farther than the next-best attempt.

Greece won several events in these Games as well. But unlike the United States' victories, which took place before huge crowds in the new Pana-thenaic Stadium, the host country's wins occurred in remote locations. By the last day, many Greeks had lost hope of seeing one of their own do something amazing. The main event of that final day was the marathon. This 26-mile race had not been part of the ancient Olympics, but it had its roots in ancient Greek history.

In 490 BC, the Persian army invaded the Greek city of Marathon. Marathon was within striking distance of Athens, the most powerful city in Greece. If Marathon fell, Athens wouldn't be far behind; if Athens fell, Greece's supremacy in the ancient world would be over. The Greeks defeated the invaders, however. According to legend, a swift Greek soldier, possibly named Pheidippedes, ran the entire 26 miles between Marathon and Athens without stopping, and then announced the victory at Marathon, collapsed, and died. Since then, a race of great distance has been called a "marathon."

The 1896 marathon replayed that first ancient run. Twenty-five runners gathered in Marathon and at the sound of the starting gun, took off for the stadium in Athens. A Frenchman took an early lead, only to drop out halfway through. An Englishman then sped into first place — but he fell out near the eighteen-mile mark, too exhausted to continue.

Meanwhile, at the stadium, King George and the other spectators awaited word of the race's progress. One hour passed. Then another.

Suddenly, a man on horseback thundered into the arena. "Louis is in the lead!" he cried joyfully.

Spyridon Louis was a twenty-five-year-old Greek shepherd. Mustachioed and slight in stature, he had trained for this race by running the course time and again. Now it appeared his hard work would pay off.

As the remaining miles passed beneath Louis's feet — feet shod in shoes donated by villagers from his hometown — the Greeks in the stadium buzzed with excitement. Would a local boy win the most talked-about event of these Games?

Two hours, fifty-eight minutes, and fifty seconds after he left Marathon, Louis staggered into the Panathenaic Stadium and, amidst deafening cheers, crossed the finish line. It would be seven minutes before another runner would follow.

"That hour was something unimaginable," Louis

remembered years later, "and it still appears to me in my memory like a dream. . . . Everybody was calling out my name and throwing their hats in the air."

Louis's victory sparked increased interest in the Games around the globe. Unfortunately, that spark soon began to fizzle. In the next twelve years, there would be three Olympics — all of them more than five and a half months long! With week-long lapses between competitions, people lost interest; in fact, many of the athletes themselves were forced to head home before their final events played out!

If the Olympics were to continue, they needed a hero. They got one in 1912.

When Native American Jim Thorpe was born, his parents named him Wa Tho Huck, which means Bright Path. And the boy certainly had a bright path ahead of him. By his early twenties, he had thrilled the world of college football with his outstanding skill. Now, at the Olympics in Stockholm, Sweden, he would amaze the international sports world with his track and field achievements.

Thorpe entered two of the most strenuous events, the pentathlon and the decathlon. The decathlon is a ten-part track and field contest consisting of the 100-meter dash, the long jump, the shot put, the high jump, the 400-meter dash, the 110-meter hurdles, the discus, the pole vault, the javelin, and the 1,500-meter race. The pentathlon has half as many parts but is no less arduous. In both cases, points are awarded to each competitor after each part; the athlete with the most points wins.

Thorpe won an easy victory in the pentathlon, taking first place in all but the javelin. Up next was the decathlon. In a driving rain that turned the outdoor track slick with mud, Thorpe came in second in both the 100-meter dash and the long jump but won the shot put to lead in points. After the second day, he was still in the lead, having won the high jump and the hurdles and placing fourth in the 400-meter run. Day three, the final day of the decathlon and of the Olympics, he tore up the track in the 1,500-meter run but showed his inexperience in the discus, pole vault, and javelin. Still, when the points were tallied, Thorpe had an amazing 8,413 out of a possible 10,000 — 688 more than the second-place winner, Hugo Wieslander of Sweden.

That afternoon, Thorpe received two crowns of laurel leaves and two gold medals from King Gustav of Sweden. After presenting Thorpe with the second set of awards, the king reached out his hand, saying, "You, sir, are the greatest athlete in the world."

Thorpe shuffled his feet, not sure of the proper response. Then he shook Gustav's hand and simply said, "Thanks, King."

Unfortunately, those hoping to follow in Thorpe's footsteps had to set aside their dreams, for in 1916, the most powerful nations in the world were embroiled in war.

In ancient times, warring city-states put down their weapons to participate in the Games. But the modern world was a much different place. Cultural, economic, and religious differences often found countries pitted against one another in struggles for supremacy. In 1914, one such struggle led to World War I, a crippling conflict that lasted four long years. The 1916 Olympic Games scheduled to take place in Berlin, Germany, were canceled in the midst of the international strife.

This was the first time politics would interfere with the Games. It would not be the last. In the years that followed, other wars, political conflicts, and beliefs in how humans should live in the world left their marks on the Olympics. Sometimes nations boycotted the Games as a way of protesting how other governments were running their countries. Sometimes the International Olympic Committee (IOC) voted to ban a nation because of that nation's politics. And sometimes, individuals protested at the Olympics to bring attention to causes that were important to them.

Luckily, the Olympic Games have survived every one of these incidents, returning to the world of sport just as they did after World War I.

★ CHAPTER THREE ★

1920–1928

New Traditions and New Games

"We swear that we will take part in these Olympic Games in the true spirit of sportsmanship, and that we will respect and abide by the rules that govern them, for the glory of sport and the honor of our country."

This Olympic Oath, written by Baron Pierre de Coubertin, was first spoken at the 1920 Olympics in Antwerp, Belgium. Belgian athlete Victor Boin recited them on behalf of all participating athletes. As he did, he held the corner of the new Olympic flag.

While the wording of the Oath has changed slightly over time, the flag's design has not. It consists of five interlocking rings — one blue, one yellow, one black, one green, one red — against a field of white. The rings represent the five areas of the world that accept and abide by the Olympic ideals; namely, the Americas, Europe, Asia, Africa, and Australia. The colors were chosen because at least one is found on the national flag of every participating country. There is no flag of the planet Earth, but perhaps the Olympic flag comes close.

The 1920 Olympics was a feast of international athletic accomplishments. From Italy came fencer Nedo Nadi, whose darting sword and dancing feet earned him six gold medals in the course of his career. Runner Paavo Nurmi brought honor to Finland by taking first place in three long-distance races and second place in a fourth. In future Games, Nurmi would add five more gold medals, making him one of only four athletes in history to earn nine Olympic gold medals.

Women did well at these Olympics, too. From France came female tennis phenom Suzanne Lenglen. Lenglen played ten sets of singles tennis in her quest for Olympic gold — and unbelievably, lost only four games. Springboard diver Aileen Riggin of the United States faced an interesting challenge: Instead of a crystal clear pool, she had to dive into a muddy-bottomed moat filled with frigid water!

"I kept thinking, the water is black and nobody could find me if I really got stuck down there," she recalled later. Fortunately for her team, she overcame her fear and took home a gold medal.

The 1920 Olympics was the last time winter and summer sports were held together. In 1921, the IOC voted to hold an "International Winter Sports Week" in Chamonix, France, in January of 1924. This week was later renamed the First Winter Olympics.

The decision to split summer and winter sporting events into two separate Games made sense. The Olympics had grown dramatically since 1896. That year, fourteen nations had sent 241 athletes to compete in forty-three events. For the 1924 Summer Games, 3,089 athletes from forty-four nations arrived in Paris, France, to take part in 126 events!

Public interest had grown too; one thousand journalists covered the action, a sure sign that people around the world wanted up-to-the-minute information on how their country's athletes were faring.

The 1924 Summer Games saw the adoption of the Olympic motto, "Citius, Altius, Fontius," meaning "Swifter, Higher, Stronger." The closing ceremonies featured a new tradition with the raising of three flags: one for the IOC, one for the current host country, and one for the next Games' host nation.

And as in the past, spectators witnessed thrilling competition by remarkable athletes. Johnny Weiss-muller of the United States swam his way to one bronze and three gold medals — and later, into the hearts and homes of thousands of Americans as the star of several Tarzan movies. English sprinter Harold Abrahams would also gain fame onscreen when his successful quest for gold was retold in the 1981 hit movie *Chariots of Fire*. Benjamin Spock helped his crew team row to a gold medal — and then, as Dr. Spock, went on to author a famous book on how to raise children.

In 1928, St. Moritz, Switzerland, hosted the second Winter Olympics. The eight-day competition included one of the strangest cross-country ski races ever. The 50-kilometer event began in subzero temperatures — but by its end, the thermostat had shot up to nearly eighty degrees! Most skiers were forced to drop out due to slushy conditions. The winning time of four hours, fifty-two minutes was a full hour longer than that achieved in the previous Olympics.

Warm temperatures ruined some outside skating events, too. But fortunately, the ice was frozen during the women's figure skating competition. If it hadn't been, the world might not have met Sonja Henie. From the moment she sailed onto the ice, the tiny blond Norwegian captivated judges and audiences alike. Six of the seven judges gave her top marks for her graceful routine, and she skated away with her first gold medal.

The 1928 Summer Games in Amsterdam, Holland, saw the introduction of two more Olympic Opening Ceremony traditions. From 1928 on, the nations would always parade in with Greece first and the host nation last. The second tradition was the lighting of the Olympic Flame. While the Flame was never a part of the ancient Olympics, its light symbolizes the ancient and honored Olympic ideal of peace between people of different nations. Once lit, the Flame stays alive for the duration of the Games.

The 1928 Summer Games recorded a few notable athletic firsts, too. Triple jumper Mikio Oda of Japan became the first Asian man to win a gold medal in an individual event. Oda became an instant hero in Japan and, in 2000, was posthumously named the Athlete of the Century by his country.

For the first time ever, women were allowed to compete in gymnastics and track and field events. Sixteen-year-old Elizabeth Robinson won the premier track event, the 100-meter dash, besting her next-closest opponent by half a meter. Robinson's promising career nearly ended three years later, when she was in a plane crash. She survived the crash, but her rescuer, believing she was dead, put her body in the trunk of his car and almost suffocated her! Amazingly, Robinson survived her ordeal, and in 1936 returned to the Olympics and helped her team win the 4x100-meter relay.

In the months that followed these Games, the

world enjoyed peace and success. Then, on October 28, 1929, the stock market crashed. Almost overnight, people around the globe were plunged into the financial disaster now known as the Great Depression. It would take more than a decade for the world to recover. Yet in the midst of financial ruin, there was one shining light — the 1932 Olympics.

★ CHAPTER FOUR ★

1932–1936

Babe and Jesse

The 1932 Winter Games took place in a tiny New York hamlet called Lake Placid. The location wasn't the only thing that was small; because of the Depression, fewer than twenty nations and three hundred athletes participated. Still, size wasn't everything, as diminutive figure skater Sonja Henie proved when she glided, twirled, and jumped her way to a second gold medal.

A few months later, at the Summer Games in Los Angeles, California, another young woman dazzled spectators. Her name was Mildred "Babe" Didrikson. Babe was the sixth of seven children born to Norwegian immigrants. According to one story, she earned her nickname during a sandlot baseball game, when the boys she was playing with said she batted like Babe Ruth.

Baseball wasn't the only sport Babe excelled at. She ran, dove, swam, boxed, cycled, bowled, and played basketball, softball, tennis, volleyball, and golf. In fact, when asked once if there was anything she didn't play, she quipped, "Yeah, dolls."

Babe once said that even before she reached her teens, she knew what she wanted to be: "My goal was to be the greatest athlete that ever lived."

Before the Olympics, she went a far distance toward reaching that goal. During the track and field meet that determined her eligibility for the Games, she placed first in six out of ten events, single-handedly outscoring entire teams!

At the Olympics, Babe took first place easily in the 80-meter hurdles and set a world record at the same time. She earned gold again in the javelin, but that medal came with a cost. As she hurled the spear, she tore cartilage in her shoulder — a painful fact that she revealed only after her opponents had taken their turns. She nearly won a third gold medal in the high jump but instead was awarded second place. The judges deemed her final jump illegal because her head had cleared the bar before the rest of her body. No one had ever bothered to tell Babe that that jumping style was illegal, however, and later, the judges awarded her a tie with first place.

Sadly, Babe's Olympic career was cut short when her image was used in an automobile ad. Babe hadn't taken money for the ad, but even so, she was forced to give up her amateur status — and thus her chances of entering any future Olympics. Some athletes might have been crushed by such a turn-around, but not Babe. She pursued a very successful golf career; at the time of her death in 1956, she achieved her teenage goal by being named the greatest female athlete of the past fifty years.

Before Babe, many people thought women were incapable of succeeding in track and field. With her victories, Didrikson proved their sexist views wrong. Four years later, a man would disprove a similar theory involving race.

In 1936, Adolf Hitler was the Reich Chancellor of

Germany. He used his power to promote his Nazi regime's agenda, which held that the Aryan race (white, blue-eyed, blond-haired people) were superior to all other races, particularly people of Jewish descent and people of color. Now Hitler had the chance to showcase his agenda to the world, for Berlin was hosting the 1936 Summer Games.

History remembers Hitler as a madman, but he wasn't stupid. Just before the Games, he toned down his anti-Semitic and racist propaganda just enough to appease critics of his philosophy. After all, he reasoned, the inferiority of non-Aryans would be aptly demonstrated when the Games commenced.

At the Opening Ceremonies, Hitler marched through the stadium behind the black swastika of his country's Nazi flag. Then a runner carrying the Olympic torch entered the stadium for the final lap of the first ever torch relay. Those images were caught on film and broadcast onto twenty-five big screens in a nearby village. This was the first time the Olympics — or any other sporting event — had ever been broadcast on live television.

Spectators and athletes in the stadium watched, too. Among them was a young African American runner named Jesse Owens.

James Cleveland Owens was one of ten children and the grandson of slaves. When Owens was a teenager, he and his family moved out of the South to Ohio. It was in school there that he got his nickname, Jesse, when a teacher misunderstood him when he said his initials were J.C. At that same school, Owens's speed caught the eye of a physical education teacher. The man encouraged Jesse to take up track and field, thus setting Owens on the path that eventually led him to the Olympics.

"I was very fortunate as a kid, meeting individuals who took an interest in me," Owens said later in life.

Owens's first event was the men's 100-meter sprint. When the starting gun cracked, he took off, arms pumping and long, muscular legs flashing in a furious blur. He crossed the finish line in 10.3 seconds, a time that tied the world record and earned him his first gold medal. Teammate Ralph Metcalfe, who was also black, took second place.

Next up was the long jump. Owens nearly disqualified himself from this event, first by wearing a sweatshirt over his uniform and then by moving beyond the takeoff line before his jump. One more misstep and he would have been out.

As Owens prepared himself for his third and final attempt, another athlete, Luz Long, tapped him on the shoulder. Long was a fellow long jumper — and a German. For him to approach Owens in front of so many was daring, even risky, given Hitler's views. Long didn't care. He wanted his rival to get the chance he deserved.

"You should be able to qualify with your eyes closed," Owens recalled Long saying. "Why don't you draw a line a few inches in back of the takeoff line and aim your takeoff from there?"

Owens took this advice — and succeeded in passing the qualifying distance by several centimeters! And in the final round, he jumped even farther, setting a world record with a distance of just over eight meters. Long was the first person to congratulate him, an act of bravery Owens never forgot. "You can melt down all the medals and cups I have and they wouldn't be a plating on the 24-karat friendship I felt for Luz Long at that moment," he once said.

In the days that followed, Owens earned two more gold medals. The first was an easy victory and a new world record in the 200-meter dash with a time of 20.7 seconds. The second, however, ignited controversy among his teammates.

The 400-meter relay took place on the eighth day of the Olympics. At the last minute, the United States coach replaced two Jewish runners, Marty Glickman and Sam Stoller, with Owens and Metcalfe. Was it possible, people wondered, that the coach held the same anti-Semitic views as Hitler?

Not likely, especially since he had put two black runners in the Jewish runners' places. Still, the change got people buzzing angrily. Not even the record-setting victory in the event quieted them completely.

For his part, Jesse Owens didn't take sides. "I wanted no part of politics," he said later. "The purpose of the Olympics was to do your best. . . . The only victory that counts is the one over yourself."

Yet Owens's triumphs, and those of other non-Aryan athletes in those Olympics, did have a huge political impact. They were no less than a triumph over Hitler and his racist agenda. Sadly, Hitler was able to downplay this very public defeat, and in the coming years, his power and influence grew immensely. In 1939, he ordered his army to invade Poland, an act of aggression that sparked World War II — and forced the cancellation of the next two Olympic Games.

CHAPTER FIVE

1948–1956

War-Torn Olympics

The Games of 1940 and 1944 were both canceled because of World War II. Peace finally prevailed in 1945. Slowly, citizens around the globe rebuilt their lives while governments worked to reestablish relationships with other countries.

The Olympics, with their ideals of peace and sportsmanship, played a part in easing tensions. The 1948 Winter Games in St. Moritz, Switzerland, were dubbed the Games of Renewal, and indeed they brought a feeling of hope to many war-torn nations. The Summer Games in London showed the world a great city still dealing with the ruins of war, but putting as bright a face on the situation as possible.

The top medal winner of the London Games was Fanny Blankers-Koen. Blankers-Koen had first competed in the Olympics in 1936 as a mediocre eighteen-year-old high jumper. That year, the highlight for her was getting Jesse Owens's autograph. Twelve years later, the Dutch runner hoped to do better in her events. But many grumbled that she didn't even belong at the Olympics because she was thirty years old and the mother of two. Critics said she'd be better off staying at home than trying to compete with younger, childless women.

That sort of talk was just what Blankers-Koen needed to spur her to victory.

And victorious she was, taking gold in the 100-meter, the 200-meter, and the 80-meter hurdles! She also earned a fourth gold as the anchor for her team's 400-meter relay. With that victory, she became the first woman ever to earn four gold medals in a single Olympics.

Many years later, at the 1972 Games in Munich, she chanced to meet up with Jesse Owens. When she introduced herself, he said, "You don't have to tell me who you are; I know everything about you."

That, Blankers-Koen said, was as incredible a moment for her as each of her gold medal wins.

Other standout athletes of the 1948 Games included Bob Mathias, who at age seventeen became the youngest male to win the Olympic decathlon. "I never worked so long and so hard for anything in my life," Mathias said, later adding that he "wouldn't do it again for a million dollars."

Karoly Takacs of Hungary gained applause not just for his shooting ability but for his amazing comeback story. During the war, Takacs's right hand — his shooting hand — was blown apart by a grenade. Many people might never have recovered from such a horrifying and disabling injury. Takacs, however, taught himself to shoot with his left hand and, ten years after the accident, won a gold medal in the rapid-fire pistol event!

Yet for all the hope felt during these Games, there were sobering reminders of the war. Chief among these were the missing athletes, such as Luz Long, who had lost their lives fighting for their countries, or who didn't compete because they had lost their edge, or who had been forced to leave sports behind during the twelve-year Olympic hiatus. Also missing were Germany and Japan, both barred from the Olympics because of their part in the war. The newly created United Soviet Socialist Republic (USSR) chose not to attend the 1948 Games.

That nation stayed away from the 1952 Winter Games as well. Its absence was not unexpected. Ever since the end of the World War II, the USSR had closed itself to countries that did not agree with its system of government. But the Soviets hadn't abandoned the Olympics. When they returned for the 1952 Summer Games in Helsinki, Finland, it seemed they had a different understanding of what the Olympics were all about. For the Soviets, winning — and winning big — was what mattered.

In fact, even before the 1952 Summer Games opened, the Soviets seemed to thumb their noses at the Olympic ideal of amateur athletic competition strengthening international ties. First, they refused to let the torch relay pass through the Soviet Union. Then they insisted that their athletes be housed separately from all others — and ringed their facilities with barbed wire fences.

Fortunately, the achievements of individual athletes shifted attention from growing political tensions between the West and the East to sports.

The most impressive performance came from a long-distance runner from Czechoslovakia. In 1948, Emil Zátopek won the gold in the 10,000-meter run and the silver in the 5,000-meter. According to one story, he was so disappointed to have missed that second gold medal that he ran at least ten miles every day for the next four years wearing heavy army boots!

True or not, whatever Zátopek did between 1948 and 1952 paid off. He won the 10,000-meter race, and then sprinted from fourth place to first in the final lap of the 5,000-meter for a second gold. Then he decided to enter the marathon — despite never having run one before!

"Do you really think that you can win your first marathon?" someone asked when word got out.

"If I didn't think I could win," Zátopek replied, "I would not have entered."

And win he did, a full two minutes ahead of the

Mildred "Babe" Didrikson, far right, hurdles her way into the record books with a best-ever time of 11.8 seconds in the 80-meter race in 1932.

Thanks to some sound advice from rival long jumper Luz Long, Jesse Owens flies into history in 1936 with a record-setting jump of 26 feet, 5 1/2 inches. That record stood for twenty-four years.

In 1960, Wilma Rudolph captivated the world with her grace, speed, and an amazing story of recovery from a paralyzing childhood disease. Here, she's sprinting the final lap of the 4x100-meter relay, on her way to a gold medal.

Mark Spitz, foreground, earned seven gold medals in the 1972 Olympics, the most any athlete had won in a single Games. Here, he's surging to the lead in the butterfly, his signature stroke.

In 1976, Romanian gymnast Nadia Comaneci scored the first-ever perfect 10—the first of several she earned in these Olympics— wowing judges with such moves as this dismount off the uneven bars.

The 1980 Winter Olympics in Lake Placid, New York, saw the underdog team from the USA beating the USSR and Czechoslovakia to win the gold—a feat better known as the Miracle on Ice. Here, they celebrate after the game-winning goal by Jim Craig against the Soviets.

In one of the most emotional moments in recent Olympic history, former Olympian and boxing great Muhammad Ali lights the Flame that signals the start of the 1996 Summer Games in Atlanta, Georgia.

The newest breed of Olympian: American snowboarder Shaun "The Flying Tomato" White amazes the judges with the height and difficulty of his move. He won gold in the halfpipe in 2006.

second-place runner! Zátopek's reaction? "The marathon is a very boring race."

Zátopek's performance was an Olympic first: no one else, then or since, has taken gold medals in the 10,000-meter, 5,000-meter, and the marathon in a single Olympics.

There were plenty of other remarkable achievements that year as well. Despite vowing he'd never compete in the decathlon again, Bob Mathias entered and won a second time. He became the only person to take successive gold medals in that event. Karoly Takacs, the right-handed shooter turned lefty, won his event again as well. And in a heartwarming tale of success over adversity, Danish equestrian Lis Hartel became one of the first women to ride dressage — the art of guiding a horse through precise maneuvers — in the Olympics, despite being paralyzed below the knees by a bout of polio years earlier. Hartel won the silver that year, and again four years later.

The United States left Helsinki happy with seventy-six medals, forty of which were gold. Their

Soviet counterparts had seventy-one medals, twenty-two of which were gold, and they left Helsinki even more determined to best their capitalist rivals in the future.

And that's just what they did in the 1956 Winter Olympics in Cortina D'Ampezzo, Italy. The Soviets ruled speed skating, cross-country skiing, and ice hockey with seven gold, three silver, and five bronze medals in these events. They also won a bronze in alpine skiing. The United States, by comparison, won only seven medals total, five of which were for figure skating.

The most notable competitor of these Winter Games didn't come from either of these countries, however. Twenty-year-old Alpine skier Anton "Toni" Sailer hailed from Austria. As a teen, Sailer had been a cautious skier. Then he watched Olympic skier Christian Pravda tear up the slopes at the 1952 Olympics, and decided it was time to change his style.

"You cannot win if you are not ready to lose," he once said.

And he lived by those words. He set records in the giant slalom and the slalom. Another win in the downhill seemed certain. But just before his race, he broke a binding. Luckily, the Italian ski coach loaned him a replacement — and moments later, Sailer flew down the hill and into the history books, the first skier to win gold in all three Alpine events in a single Olympics.

In the years that followed, politics continued to play a major role in the Olympics. Governments with differing philosophies clashed time and again; in some cases, these clashes led nations to boycott the Games, a very public protest against opposing political views.

Yet athletes continued to meet and mingle every four years. In 1956, an Olympic closing ceremony tradition was born. In contrast to the opening ceremonies, where all participating nations parade in separately, the closing ceremonies found the nations entering the stadium en masse. For that short time, at least, peoples with differing politics, religions, customs, and cultures joined together in the truest spirit of the Olympic ideals.

★ CHAPTER SIX ★

1960–1968

Protests Amidst the Games

At most Winter Olympics, it's the downhill skiing, figure skating, and speed skating events that make headlines. But in 1960, it was the ice hockey final that grabbed people's attention.

The United States had unexpectedly powered its way past the USSR and Canada to face Czechoslovakia in the finals. But then it seemed the underdog had met its match. At the end of the second period, the US was down 4–3.

Then, during the intermission, Soviet hockey player Nikolai Sologubov came into the United States' locker room. Using sign language, Sologubov suggested that the tired players use oxygen to rejuvenate themselves. Team USA took the suggestion — and it worked. The Americans stormed back to take the gold medal with a final score of 9–4. No one knows exactly why Sologubov aided his rivals, but some believe he wanted to see the Czechs lose, even if it meant the Americans won.

These Games also saw television being put to a new use. When judges couldn't agree whether a skier had missed a gate during his slalom run, they reviewed a recording of his run — the first instant replay.

Fewer than seven hundred athletes took part in the 1960 Winter Olympics. Six months later, nearly five times that many showed up for the Summer Olympics in Rome. Among them was a woman with astonishing athletic ability — and an equally astonishing story of determination.

When Wilma Rudolph was a child, she was stricken with scarlet fever, polio, and double pneumonia. Any one of these diseases could have killed her; polio could have left her paralyzed. But Rudolph beat them all to become one of the greatest female runners of all time.

At age sixteen, Rudolph won a bronze medal as part of the 400-meter relay team in the 1956 Olympics.

Now, at age twenty, she left the competition in the dust. First, she won the 100-meter dash a full three meters ahead of the second-place runner. She took her second gold medal three days later in the 200-meter dash. And lastly, she anchored the gold medal–winning team in the 400-meter relay.

Rudolph's victories were a personal triumph and an inspiration for female athletes of all ages. For years, track and field events were considered un-feminine. But Rudolph ran with such grace that she earned the nickname "The Black Gazelle."

"People saw her as beauty in motion," her coach, Nell Jackson, later recalled.

"Beauty in motion" was how another Olympian might have described himself. Cassius Clay was a confident boxer and in 1960, he pummeled his way to his first gold medal, besting the much-favored Zbigniew Pietrzykowski of Poland. Clay didn't compete in the Olympics again, but he is still the best-known boxer in the world. Of course, the world knows him by a different name: Muhammad Ali.

For many years, the site of upcoming Olympics was chosen well in advance, so that the host city and country could prepare for the huge influx of athletes and spectators. But in the days before the 1964 Winter Games, Innsbruck, Austria, had to scramble to complete its preparations, for their slopes lacked a very important element: snow! The weather prior to the Games had been unseasonably warm and the mountainsides were nearly bare.

Fortunately, the Austrian army saved the day. They moved ice and snow from nearby mountains and hand-packed it onto the ski, bobsled, and luge courses. By Opening Day, everything was up and running.

As usual, the USSR took top honors in these Games. Leading the charge was female speed skater Lidiya Skoblikova. She swept aside the competition and won gold medals in all four events, including the first-ever women's 500-meter race. This achievement set a new Winter Olympic record, and when added to the two first-place medals she had won in 1960, made her the first winter athlete and only female ever to win six gold medals in individual events.

Another first was the awarding of the De Coubertin Medal for sportsmanship. Named for the baron who had resurrected the Olympics, the medal was first awarded to bobsleigher Eugenio Monti of Italy. When the rival team from Great Britain needed a replacement axle bolt for their sleigh, Monti loaned them one of his.

"As far as I was concerned," Monti said later, "[they] would have done the same for me." Great Britain's team took the gold. Monti's took the bronze.

In August, the Summer Olympics traveled to its first Asian locale, Tokyo, Japan. Competition was as fierce as ever — and as in years past, the tightest contests were between the USA and the USSR. This time around, Team USA won the battle, earning thirty-six gold, twenty-six silver, and twenty-eight bronze medals. They dominated the men's athletics events, taking fourteen firsts in track and field.

Still, the Soviets won thirty gold, thirty-one silver, and thirty-five bronze awards, many of them in gymnastics, a field they would own for several Olympics to come. Their top athlete in this category was a thirty-year-old woman competing in her third Olympics.

Larissa Latynina was already beloved in her native

country of Ukraine. Going into the 1964 Games, her combined Olympic medal total stood at seven golds, three silvers, and two bronzes. By the end of those Games, she had added two more of each. Her nineteen medals are the most any Olympic athlete has ever won. Whether competing on the vault, uneven bars, balance beam, or floor, her grace, agility, athleticism, and versatility were unparalleled at the time.

When it came to competing in the Olympics, it was natural for athletes to want to do all they could to win. Unfortunately, at the 1968 Winter Olympics in Grenoble, France, one group of athletes found victory through cheating. The East German women's single luge team heated their runners to make their luges move faster over the ice. When the cheating was discovered, the team was forced to give over their first-, second-, and fourth-place positions.

Another, more bizarre incident of foul play occurred on the slopes. Austrian slalom skier Karl Schranz reported that during his run, a man dressed in black had crossed in front of him, causing him to skid to a halt. No one else had seen the man because the course was shrouded in fog. Still, the judges gave Schranz the benefit of the doubt and allowed him a restart. Schranz's make-up run was so good it beat the time of lead skier and local hero Jean-Claude Killy.

Killy didn't take the challenge sitting down, however. He contested the judges' decision to give Schranz a second chance — and won his appeal. Schranz's first place was disqualified and Killy declared the winner.

The 1968 Summer Olympics had its share of controversies, too, starting with the location. Mexico City has a very high altitude and thus a much lower oxygen level than some other cities. Anyone not acclimated to the thinner air risked suffering from headaches, nausea, and sleeplessness. Athletes who were used to the altitude, on the other hand, had an undue advantage. Despite this concern, the Olympics took place in Mexico City as planned. And in the end, the question of altitude took a back seat to other issues.

Many areas of the world were in upheaval in 1968. Students were rioting in Paris, France, over unfair wages. Czechoslovakia had been invaded by the USSR. In the United States, the assassinations of Martin Luther King, Jr. and presidential candidate Robert Kennedy highlighted the escalating violence of the civil rights movement. Ten days before the Summer Games, hundreds of Mexican students were killed while protesting against their government.

The 1968 Games opened against this backdrop of unrest. While many athletes chose to concentrate on sports rather than politics, some decided to use the very public arena of the Games to express their opinions.

The most memorable of these events took place during the medal ceremony for the 200-meter race. With "The Star-Spangled Banner" playing, African Americans Tommie Smith and John Carlos stepped onto the first- and third-place podiums — and showed their anger to the world.

Both were in their stocking feet, a protest against the poverty of African Americans. Both had civil rights buttons attached to their uniforms, a show of support for that cause. Smith wore a black scarf and Carlos wore black beads to symbolize the horrifying crime of lynching. Then Smith and Carlos bowed their heads and raised black-gloved fists into the air in the Black Power salute. "It was not a gesture of hate, but frustration," Smith later told the press.

Today, their passive protest against racial discrimination may seem tame, but back then it sent shockwaves through those who understood the significance of their actions. The IOC immediately suspended the two men and barred them from the Olympic Village.

In the midst of such protests came several outstanding athletic achievements. High jumper Dick Fosbury introduced the Fosbury Flop, an innovative new technique for clearing the bar backdown rather than facedown. Fellow American Bob Beamon broke the long jump record by more than half a meter. Czech gymnast Vera Caslavska raised her Olympic medal total from three gold and two silver in 1964 to seven gold and four silver in 1968 — despite having been forced to flee during the Soviet invasion of her country earlier in the year.

The Olympics of 1968 were among the most politically controversial to date. But the protests made during these Games were nothing next to what happened four years later.

★ CHAPTER SEVEN ★

1972–1976

"The Games Must Go On!"

The 1972 Winter Olympics in Sapporo, Japan, passed with little political intrigue. Then came the Summer Games of 1972.

Germany played host for the first time since Hitler's Olympics in 1936. In the hopes of erasing the memory of those long-ago Games, the city of Munich pulled out all the stops. At the Opening Ceremony, German president Gustav Heinemann said he hoped these Olympics would be "a milestone on the road to a new way of life with the aim of realizing peaceful coexistence among peoples."

At first, it appeared that Heinemann's hopes would be met. The Games were progressing smoothly, with many new world records set and astonishing athletic performances seen. Swimmer Mark Spitz slashed through the waves to an Olympic record of seven gold medals and seven world records. Seventeen-year-old Russian gymnast Olga Korbut catapulted to fame, charming the world with her bright smile, emotion-packed routines, unbelievable flexibility, and daring moves.

"It was amazing," the Belarus native recalled later. "One day I was a nobody, and the next day I was a star."

Korbut, Spitz, and others made headlines in these Olympics — but only one story was front-page news.

On September 5th at 4:30 a.m., a group of six masked men climbed over the fence into the Olympic Village. They carried duffel bags filled with grenades and guns. Two others joined them and together they crept to the Israeli team's quarters.

Inside Apartment 1, a burly wrestling referee named Yossef Gutfreund was awakened by a strange scratching sound. Suddenly, he saw a masked man armed with a gun entering his quarters!

Gutfreund shouted warnings to his roommates and then hurled himself against the door. One Israeli escaped through a window. Another, wrestling coach Moshe Weinberg, fought the intruders with Gutfreund.

The gunman shot Weinberg through the cheek and subdued Gutfreund. The other terrorists took more hostages from Apartment 3. Weinberg attacked again. This time, the intruders killed him — but not before Weinberg had wounded one man and left another unconscious. Another Israeli was also killed. Nine more were taken hostage and held at gunpoint by the masked men.

The terrorists were members of a Palestinian organization called Black September. In exchange for the Israeli athletes, they demanded the release of two hundred Palestinian prisoners and other sympathizers jailed in Israel. There would be no negotiation.

The media covering the Games immediately turned their cameras on the crisis. While those cameras alerted the world of what was happening, they also contributed to a failed rescue attempt. Television crews broadcast live footage of German police disguised as competitors entering the Village. The Palestinians simply followed the officers' progress on TV and then threatened to kill hostages when the officers drew near. The officers had no choice but to back off.

Tragically, death came to hostage and captor alike.

Jim McKay, sportscaster for the ABC network, broke the news: "Our worst fears have been realized tonight. They've now said that there were eleven hostages; two were killed in their rooms yesterday morning, nine were killed at the airport tonight. They're all gone."

The Olympics were immediately suspended. Flags were flown at half-mast and a memorial service held for the victims. Heinemann's wish for "peaceful co-existence" had died, too.

But then, in a move aimed at showing the world that the Olympics would not bow down beneath cowardly acts of terrorism, IOC president Avery Brundage made an announcement.

"The Games must go on!"

So, twenty-four hours later, the final events of the 1972 Olympics were played out. And four years later, the Games returned with renewed vigor — and greatly increased security.

Denver, Colorado, had been chosen as the site for the 1976 Winter Games. The residents of Colorado had other ideas, however. Concerned that so much construction in their state would cause irreparable damage to the environment, they voted not to host. Fortunately, Innsbruck, Austria, was willing to open its doors again. In honor of that city's assistance, a second Olympic flame was lit during the Opening Ceremonies.

These games introduced the world to nineteen-year-old Dorothy Hamill. Hamill captured her audience's hearts with her stunning grace. But it was her signature move, the Hamill Camel, that convinced the judges to unanimously award her the gold medal. The move began with a camel spin, in which she pulled one leg up into an arabesque position and twirled on the other leg. From here, she dropped straight down into a sit spin.

These Games also saw the most amazing downhill ski run in Olympic history. Going into his final run, Austrian Franz Klammer was behind two other skiers by a wide enough margin that besting them seemed impossible.

But Klammer didn't give up. Dressed in a bright yellow ski suit, he catapulted out of the starting gate. One-third through the 3,145-meter course, he was still behind the two lead skiers' times. Two-thirds of the way through, he needed to make up more than a fifth of a second. He had to do something drastic.

He did. At a place in the course known as Bear's Neck, he streaked on a straight line rather than curving. It was an incredibly risky move, one that would have felled many skiers and nearly sent him into a group of spectators.

Klammer stayed in control, though his knees were hammering as his skis pounded over the frozen slope. One tiny misstep now and he would end his breakneck run in a twist of limbs, skis, and poles. But the yellow figure just kept going and when he crossed the finish line, he had a new world record and an Olympic gold! His official speed was the best in Olympic history at the time, an amazing 102.828 kilometers per hour.

The Olympics traveled across the Atlantic to Montreal, Canada, for the Summer Games of 1976. Sadly, twenty-seven nations from Africa and the

Middle East chose not to attend. These nations had asked the IOC to ban New Zealand for that country's apparent approval of South Africa's apartheid government — a system of legal racial discrimination. When the IOC didn't honor the request, the African countries boycotted in protest.

Despite the long shadow cast by the absence of these nations, there were some sunny spots. The brightest beam emanated from a tiny gymnast from Romania named Nadia Comaneci.

Comaneci had been in training since she was five years old. Now, at age fourteen, she held the European championship title and was poised to earn gold at the Olympics. And earn it she did, with the Olympics' first-ever perfect score in gymnastics! Unbelievably, that perfect 10 on the uneven parallel bars was followed by another — and another, and another, and another, until in total she had accumulated seven perfect scores — four on the uneven bars, two on the balance beam, and one in floor exercises.

Sadly, Comaneci's life after the Olympics wasn't as perfect as her scores. Overwhelmed by her sudden fame and the grueling demands of her sport, she attempted suicide at age fifteen. She recovered, emotionally and physically, and later defected to the United States. She married gymnast Bart Conner, whom she had met briefly at the 1976 Games. Today, she and Conner are involved in several charitable organizations, including one that helps homeless children in Romania.

★ CHAPTER EIGHT ★

1980–1988

Miracles and Memorable Moments

The Olympics returned to Lake Placid, New York, in the winter of 1980. There were several standout performances by individuals, including American skater Eric Heiden, who won all five speed skating events, and Swedish Alpine skier Ingemar Stenmark, who came from behind in two different races to win two gold medals.

But without a doubt the story of the Games was the United States ice hockey team. Made up of mostly college-aged boys, this inexperienced squad wreaked havoc with the established leaders of the sport. They tied Sweden 2–2 in the first round and then rolled over Czechoslovakia, Norway, Romania, and Germany to reach the semi-finals against the Soviets.

In the first period of that game, the Soviet team outshot and outplayed the Americans. But thanks to save after save by goalkeeper Jim Craig, the United States was only behind 2–1.

Then, as the last minutes of the first period ticked by, Dave Christian took a shot. It was blocked but the rebound was picked up by Mark Johnson, who slashed it past the Soviet goalie just as the buzzer sounded!

The referees conferred to determine if the shot had struck the net before or after the end of the period. They decided the shot was good. The score was tied.

The Soviets dominated the ice again in the second period, raising their score to 3–2. During that same time, the United States had managed only two shots on goal. If the American team was to win, they'd have to bring something to the ice that the Soviets couldn't match.

That's what they did. The USSR team had finesse and experience, but the US players had speed and youth on their side and they put both — plus a little luck — to work in the first ten minutes of the third period. First Johnson sent a loose puck rocketing into the goal. Then US captain Mike Eruzione nabbed the puck off the stick of a Soviet defenseman, skated to the high slot and, using the defenseman to screen his move, blasted a 25-foot shot straight into the goal. The US now led 4–3!

Ten minutes remained. Then nine. Slowly, the clock ticked down and still the United States held onto their lead. The fans in the stands were screaming and people watching on television at home were jumping and yelling. Even the broadcasters were excited, including sports announcer Al Michaels, who delivered the now-classic countdown:

"Eleven seconds. You got ten seconds, the countdown going on right now. Five seconds left in the game! Do you believe in miracles? Yes!"

The United States went on to beat Finland 4–2 in the finals to win the gold medal. Their amazing feat, dubbed the "Miracle on Ice," captivated the sports world and has been retold many times, most recently in the movie *Miracle*.

There would be no such miracle for US athletes at the Summer Olympics in Moscow, however. In fact, there would be no US athletes at the Summer Olympics in Moscow.

The United States, under a directive from President Jimmy Carter, was boycotting the Games to protest the 1979 Soviet invasion of Afghanistan. More than sixty other nations joined the boycott, making participation at these Summer Games the lowest since 1956. For the competitors who had trained for years for their chance at gold, it was a bitter blow, and another example of politics intruding upon the world of sport.

The United States returned to the Olympics for the 1984 Winter Games in Sarajevo, Yugoslavia. There they took home a mere four gold medals: three for Alpine skiing and one for figure skating.

But it was the figure skaters from other countries who dominated the competition. From Great Britain came the dynamic ice dancing duo of Jayne Torvill and Christopher Dean. Separately, they were accomplished skaters; together, they were poetry in motion, dipping and swirling across the ice in exquisite harmony. Their artistry earned them perfect 10s from all the judges and gold medals besides.

"We weren't with the audience last night," Dean said the morning after their performance, "we were with each other."

From Germany came a talented young woman named Katarina Witt. Witt dazzled with her expressive routines, twirling, gliding, and leaping her way past the competition and into the audience's hearts. Like many other athletes, she gained great fame through the Olympics. That fame was not as important to her as the Olympic ideal, however.

"Setting a meaningful example of peaceful and humane competition to young people and other generations; promoting a contest of strength without destruction; that, for me, has been the inner heart of the Olympic Games," she once said.

In August of 1984, Los Angeles played host to the Summer Games for the second time. The first time, in 1932, thirty-seven nations and 1,332 athletes participated; in 1984, 140 nations and 6,829 athletes took part!

Among the competitors was a man who hoped to duplicate his hero's past performance. Carl Lewis of the United States had grown up admiring Jesse

Owens. Now, as the favored competitor in track and field, he would have his chance to follow in his idol's fleet footsteps.

The second day of the Games, Lewis lined up alongside teammate Sam Graddy and Canada's Ben Johnson for the 100-meter sprint. After 80 meters, Graddy was in the lead. Then, with an amazing burst of power, Lewis caught up to Graddy — and passed him, crossing the finish line a full two meters ahead of him!

Two days later, Lewis set a world record in the 200-meter dash *after* having won the gold medal in the long jump earlier in the day!

Lewis was now one gold medal away from duplicating Jesse Owens's 1936 Olympic feats. Last up was the 400-meter relay. Lewis was the anchor for his team, just as Owens had been nearly fifty years before. And like Owens before him, Lewis helped himself and his team to a gold medal with a world record time.

"I've always believed that if you work hard at whatever you want to do, you can make it," Lewis later said in an interview, adding, "Making it doesn't mean doing 'the best,' it means doing 'the best you can.'"

As remarkable as Lewis's accomplishments were, it was a wrestler from New York State who captured the hearts of many Americans in this Olympics.

Jeff Blatnick had begun his career as a freestyle wrestler in college. In 1980, he had hopes of going to the Moscow Olympics. President Carter's boycott of those Games ended that dream — and a year later, something else nearly ended his life.

Blatnick seemed in prime physical shape. Then he discovered lumps in his neck. That discovery led to a diagnosis of Hodgkin's disease. Blatnick had cancer. Fortunately, radiation and surgery cured him and three years later he was back in the ring. Still, doubts crowded his mind. Was he in good enough condition to compete against the strongest wrestlers in the world?

He wasn't just good enough, he was the best. He flattened his opponents one by one to reach the final round. As he stepped forward to begin the gold medal match, he heard his mother shout, "Do it for Dave!" referring to Jeff's brother who had died in a motorcycle accident years earlier. That cry may have given Blatnick the extra boost he needed, for he toppled Thomas Johansson of Sweden to earn the gold medal.

Television cameras then captured one of the most stirring moments in Olympic history. Blatnick, overwhelmed by emotion, fell to his knees in prayer and began to weep. When he tried to talk to reporters afterward, he couldn't.

"I'm embarrassed," he confessed later, "but I'm not ashamed. I guess it's like people always say, 'The big guys are babies.'"

On the other side of the size coin was four-foot-nine-inch gymnast Mary Lou Retton. The sixteen-year-old recalled gymnastic greats of Olympics past, including Olga Korbut and Nadia Comaneci, with one big difference: Retton was an American. After years of bowing down to the might of Soviet and Eastern European gymnasts, the United States finally had a champion. With muscular athleticism and grace, she garnered the first ever all-around gymnastics title won by Team USA.

"You're a hero," President Ronald Regan told her,

"living proof of what happens when America sets its sights high and says, 'Let's create a little excellence.'"

Excellence continued four years later at the Winter Games in Calgary, Canada, including a surprisingly competitive team of bobsleighers from tropical Jamaica whose story was later turned into the movie *Cool Runnings*. But at the 1988 Summer Games in Seoul, Korea, one man's excellence turned out to be falsely obtained.

When Toronto resident Ben Johnson exploded onto the track and field scene, all of Canada rejoiced, for their country had never produced a champion runner. Earlier in the year, Johnson had astounded people by clocking a time of 9.83 seconds in the 100-meter dash at the World Championships. Now, in the finals of the same event in Seoul, he performed a miracle, besting that time by four hundredths of a second!

How had Johnson done it? The answer to that question became painfully clear within forty-eight hours, when Johnson tested positive for performance-enhancing steroids. He was unceremoniously stripped of his gold medal. He wasn't the first — or, sadly, the last — athlete to cheat in this way, but his case brought the problem of steroid use to the public's attention. Within a year, random drug testing would become the norm for the sports world.

Fortunately, heroes usually outnumber villains at the Olympics. One such hero was American diver Greg Louganis.

As a child, Louganis had such trouble reading that his peers made fun of him. (Louganis was later diagnosed as having dyslexia, a learning disorder.) He escaped the cruel taunts by diving.

"The pool was my sanctuary," he once said.

Louganis first gained Olympic glory at the 1976 Games, where he won a silver medal in the platform; in 1984, he earned two golds, one for platform and one for springboard. Now, in 1988, he was on track to duplicate that performance.

Then something awful happened. Midway through a reverse two-and-a-half somersault pike, he hit his forehead on the springboard, and landed in the water with a huge splash. Doctors quickly stitched and bandaged the wound. But they couldn't administer any cure for his sudden plummet from first to fifth place. Louganis himself would have to tend to that.

He did, with a nearly flawless reverse one-and-a-half somersault, three-and-a-half twist dive. With that dive, he became the only person ever to win gold medals in both events in two consecutive Olympics. Still, Louganis hopes he won't be alone in accomplishing this feat.

"I don't want to be remembered as the greatest diver who ever lived," he once said. "I hope I live to see the day when my records are broken."

That hasn't happened yet, but with years of Olympic Games stretching into the future, Louganis may get his wish someday.

✷ CHAPTER NINE ✷

1992–1994

Splitting the Olympiad

The Olympics of 1992 were the last time the Summer and Winter Games were held in the same year. The Games had simply grown too massive an undertaking to be held within months of each other. So the IOC voted to move the Winter Olympics up two years, to 1994, and then to follow the typical four-year schedule thereafter. The Summer Olympics continued every four years from 1992 onward.

The star of the 1992 Winter Games in Albertville, France, was Italian Alpine skier Alberto "La Bomba" Tomba. Tomba was one of the most popular skiers ever to hit the slopes, beloved not just for his talent but for his playful attitude and handsome looks. In the Calgary Games four years earlier, he had taken home two gold medals in the slalom and giant slalom. Now he would attempt to repeat that feat.

Doing so was far from in the bag. In the four years since Calgary, Tomba's fame and wealth had distracted him from practicing as much as he should have. He won only four events in two of those years. Luckily, a new coach got him back on track. But would it be enough?

Almost.

Tomba tackled the giant slalom first. "[It] was really difficult," he confessed later. "The slope was tough at the top . . . yes, I had been pretending to be confident . . . but inside, I wasn't at all sure."

Still, he pulled through and won the event, with more than 30,000 adoring spectators cheering him on.

Three days later, the pressure was on again, this time for the slalom. If Tomba won this event, he would take home consecutive gold medals in both slalom and giant slalom, something no skier had ever done before.

Unfortunately for Tomba fans, history would not be made that day. Finn Christian Jagge of Norway bested him by 0.28 seconds. Tomba had to settle for silver.

While Tomba was tearing up the slopes, American speed skater Bonnie Blair was slashing through the rink. Blair came from a family of speed skaters; in fact, she claims that when she was born, her father was at a meet with her older siblings! Blair followed the family tradition, taking to the rink when she was just two years old and speed skating for the first time at age four. At her first Olympic appearance in 1984, she placed eighth in the 500-meter race; four years later, she earned the gold medal in that event, and in the 1,000-meter race.

Now, at age twenty-two, Blair prepared to defend her title in the 500-meter race. The starting gun blasted and she took off, her muscular legs and arms pumping in rhythm and driving her into the lead.

"Her long strides make her the best technician in the world over the sprint distance, man or woman," her coach once noted. "It's like she was born on ice."

Those long strides sent Blair across the finish line ahead of the pack, making her the first female speed skater to win consecutive gold medals in the 500-

meter race. Then they pushed her across first again in the 1,000-meter, but she was only two hundredths of a second ahead of the second-place winner.

Many athletes who make history as Blair did would boast and brag. That wasn't Blair's style. While a group of forty-five friends and family — the Blair Bunch, as they called themselves — cheered wildly, she received her medals with quiet joy.

"Bonnie doesn't know she's a celebrity," her mother, Eleanor, once said. "She sees herself as a regular person."

A regular person with five gold medals, that is, for Blair added two more in future Olympics.

Very often, the Olympic Games highlight individual achievements. But in 1992, the talk of the Summer Games in Barcelona, Spain, was about the basketball team from the United States.

This was the first year the IOC allowed professional basketball players to take part in the Olympics. While some countries had only a few players of great caliber, the National Basketball Association (NBA) of the United States had enough to fill several teams. Michael Jordan of the Chicago Bulls,

Larry Bird of the Boston Celtics, and Magic Johnson of the Los Angeles Lakers anchored the most powerful team ever to hit the Olympic courts. They didn't just win, they annihilated their competition, usually by margins of 35 to 40 points.

The 1992 Summer Games saw the return of South Africa, a country that had been banned from the competition since 1960 because of its apartheid policy. Now that policy had been overturned and, in a touching tribute to South Africa's new approach to race, black female runner Derartu Tulu of Ethiopia, and white South African runner Elana Meyer, ran a lap hand-in-hand after placing first and second in the 10,000-meter race. Their embrace afterward demonstrated just how important the Olympics were in promoting healing after long conflict.

No matter what their sport, nationality, or philosophy, all Olympic athletes are under extreme pressure. No matter how good they are going into the Games, there is always the worry that someone else will be better. Most embrace the competitive spirit and can handle the pressure, but a few have been known to crack. Ice skater Tonya Harding was one such athlete.

Harding had a troubled upbringing. Her mother supported her skating ambitions by sewing her costumes and paying for her training — but she also beat and insulted her daughter when she didn't do well. Her father forced her to chop wood and work on his pick-up truck, among other arduous tasks. In a sport that prized grace, beauty, and virtue, the chain-smoking, tough-talking Harding looked out of place.

Yet her skill was great and vaulted her into the top ranks of the figure skating world. Also in those ranks was a dark-haired girl with a winning smile named Nancy Kerrigan. Kerrigan fit the image of figure skater to a T and delighted audiences with her seemingly effortless routines.

In the weeks leading up to their 1994 Olympic showdown in Lillehammer, Norway, the press made much of their contrasting backgrounds and upcoming competition. But on January 6, the media had to cover an appalling new story about the two skaters.

Kerrigan was resting after training in Detroit, Michigan, when suddenly a man jumped out at her, clubbed her on the knee with a lead pipe, and vanished. Kerrigan crumpled to the floor, screaming in agony. That one blow put her Olympic career in jeopardy.

Authorities tracked down the man and then pieced together a shocking truth: Tonya Harding's husband had hired the attacker to eliminate Kerrigan from the competition. While it was never proven that Harding herself knew what her husband intended to do, the scandal rocked the sporting world.

As it turned out, the plot failed. Kerrigan's knee healed in time for the Olympics and while she performed beautifully, she wound up with the silver. The gold went to a young Ukrainian skater named Oksana Baiul.

The world would have to wait just two more years for the next Olympics. In 1996, the modern Games would celebrate their centenary, a milestone that was met with an explosion of celebration — as well as another, much less welcome explosion.

★ CHAPTER TEN ★

1996–2002

From Centenary Celebrations to Scandals

The Opening Ceremonies of the Olympic centenary in Atlanta, Georgia, were filled with reminders and reflections of modern Olympic history. Past athletic heroes such as Mark Spitz, Nadia Comaneci, and Carl Lewis joined 11,000 current competitors in the main stadium. Together, they and hundreds of thousands of spectators watched the final leg of the Olympic Torch Relay.

As trumpets blared and a choir sang the Olympic Anthem, swimmer Janet Evans entered the stadium, rounded the track, and strode up the ramp with the Flame. A lone figure, seen only in silhouette, stood at the top of the ramp. When Evans drew alongside him, he held out his unlit torch to her — and as she passed him the Flame, his identity was revealed.

It was Muhammad Ali, one of the greatest champions of the world of sport. The stadium erupted with thunderous applause. Ali, still muscular despite a debilitating disease that caused his hands and head to shake, touched his Torch to a fuse and stood back to watch the Flame make its final journey through the darkness to the cauldron above.

The crowd hushed. Slowly, the fire inched up the wire. At last, the flame reached the cauldron. Flames burst forth, setting the night sky aglow. Music swelled and people the world over cheered.

They would have many more opportunities to cheer in the following days, for these Olympics boasted some remarkable athletic achievements.

In the track and field arena, American runner Michael Johnson was the odds-on favorite. After all, he had held the 400-meter world championship title for seven years, winning that race more than fifty times in a row, including a victory at the 1992 Olympics. Now he defended his title easily, streaking across the finish line a whole ten meters ahead of Roger Black of Great Britain! That ten meters was the greatest margin of victory in one hundred years of the Olympics.

How did Black feel about losing by that margin? Not all that bad, as it turned out. "A silver behind Johnson is like a gold ahead of anyone else!" he said with a smile.

A few days later, Johnson won the 200-meter race, becoming the first man to take gold in both events in a single Olympics.

Carl Lewis, returning for his fourth Olympics, also made his way into the record books. When he won the long jump, he added his fourth consecutive gold medal in that event. He was one of only three athletes to win gold in his event four times — and one of only four athletes to win nine Olympic golds in his career.

But of all the athletes, one young gymnast perhaps best epitomized the Olympic spirit that year. Kerri Strug of the United States had long dreamed of earning gold at the Games. It didn't happen in 1992, her first Olympic outing, so she set her sights on Atlanta.

Going into the final day of gymnastics competition, the US team had a wide lead over the Russian squad. All they needed to do to hold that lead was deliver a solid performance on the vault.

Up first was Dominique Moceanu, the team's strongest vaulter. Unbelievably, she fell in both of her attempts. Suddenly, a US victory wasn't quite as certain.

Kerri Strug was the last to vault for her team. With the gold medal hanging in the balance, she made her run toward the horse, bounded off the springboard, and flipped through the air. The vault looked good — until she landed so hard that something in her ankle popped. Wincing in pain and holding back tears, Strug limped to the sidelines.

"I could feel the gold medal slipping away," she later told reporters.

But her coach didn't believe that. "You can do it," he told the girl.

So Strug approached the run for her last vault. Her ankle was bound securely with tape, but still she could feel pain coursing up her leg. She pushed it aside, took a deep breath, and sprinted toward the horse. She flung herself into the vault, flipping high in the air, twisting around with near-perfect form, and landing solidly on her good foot. Then she collapsed. As her coach carried her to the sidelines, her scores flashed across the boards. She had earned 9.712, more than good enough for her team to win the gold. But it was her push to do the best she could for her team that won the hearts of spectators everywhere.

Four days later, however, Strug's feat was all but forgotten. In the middle of a late-night concert in the Olympic Centennial Park, a bomb exploded. Two people were killed and 110 injured.

In the hours that followed the attack, police swarmed the area. "We will spare no effort to find out who was responsible for this murderous act," President Bill Clinton told the world. "We will track them down. We will bring them to justice."

The perpetrator, it turned out, was a man named Eric Robert Rudolph. He wanted to embarrass the United States government by shutting down the Olympics. But his plot failed, for after a period of mourning the Games continued as planned.

After the tragedy in Atlanta, security was stepped up for the 1998 Winter Games in Nagano, Japan. Fortunately, there was no recurrence of such trouble. But there was trouble for many of the Games' favored athletes. In women's figure skating, the apparent gold medalist, Michelle Kwan, was upset by her younger teammate, Tara Lipinski. The US ice hockey "Dream Team" was sent packing after losing in the quarter-finals. The once-great skier Alberto Tomba escaped to his hotel room rather than finish out his slalom run.

Snowboarding had been popular for many years but had been disdained as a sport worthy of the Olympics. Now, after much lobbying by snowboard enthusiasts, it finally appeared on the program. There were two events for women and men, the giant slalom and the halfpipe.

The sport took a shot on the chin when the winner of the men's slalom, Canadian Ross Rebagliati, was stripped of his gold when he tested positive for marijuana. Rebagliati's medal was returned to him on a technicality, but his drug use gave snowboard critics plenty of ammunition.

Sadly, allegations of drug use again made headlines two years later, during the first Olympic Games of the twenty-first century. When her husband tested positive for performance-enhancing steroids, United States runner Marion Jones came under the microscope, too. Jones had already been in the media for her "Drive for Five" ambition, a very public quest to win five gold medals in a single Olympics. Now the press followed her every move, barraging her with questions about her husband and all but accusing her of steroid use. Jones stated over and over that she was clean—statements that have since turned out to be false—and tried to focus on her events. Unfortunately, her lack of skill in the long jump left her one short of her goal.

Other Olympic quests fell just short of their goal, too. Seventeen-year-old Australian swimmer Ian Thorpe was a home-grown hero. He beat his own world record in the 400-meter freestyle and then anchored his team to victory in the 4x100-meter freestyle relay, toppling the United States' thirty-six-year winning streak in that event. He added a third gold medal in the 4x200-meter freestyle relay. But any hope of Thorpe besting other powerhouses ended in disappointment when he took silver in both the 200-meter freestyle and the 4x100-meter medley relay.

Russian Aleksandr Karelin, the top Greco-Roman wrestler for thirteen years, fell beneath the might of Rulon Gardner of the United States. Men's tri-athlete favorite Simon Lessing was defeated in his event, too.

But the top story in upsets was undoubtedly the United States women's softball team victory. Softball had first appeared at the Olympics in 1996. The United States squad won that year and now they hoped to defend their title. But when they lost three games in a row, they were on the brink of elimination. Instead, they fought their way back into the running, beating the three teams that had beaten them, and then took the gold medal by besting Japan 2–1 in eight long innings.

"What made us so happy," team captain Dot Richardson said in a later interview, "was knowing when so many others might have given up, we believed in ourselves and conquered the world. It's not the receiving of the gold medal but the journey we took in order to achieve it."

The Olympic journey's next stop was Salt Lake City, Utah. The choice of Salt Lake City had nearly been overturned when evidence proved that some IOC members had accepted bribes to cast their vote for the location. The selection stood despite this scandal and most hoped that would be the end of any problems for these Games.

It wasn't. During the Games, several athletes tested positive for drugs, further eroding the spirit of sportsmanship and fair play so vital to the Olympics. But the biggest setback of all came when a figure skating judge admitted she had given higher-than-deserved scores to a Russian pairs team. These scandals, coming as they did one on top of another, threatened the very Games themselves — for if the IOC, the athletes, and the judges were all cheating, who was left to uphold the Olympic ideals?

Luckily, for every one athlete who chose to use

drugs, there were hundreds who played by the rules. It was their hard work and exceptional performances that lifted the Games above the disgraces.

One such performance came from a sixteen-year-old figure skater named Sarah Hughes. Going into the final event, the free skate, Hughes was in fourth place behind Irina Slutskaya, Sasha Cohen, and Michelle Kwan.

The crowd was pulling for Kwan, who had unexpectedly been beaten by Tara Lipinski in 1996. But she made two critical errors during her routine and dropped down to second. Slutskaya's high-scoring performance pushed Kwan even further behind. Cohen was out of the running by this time, which brought up Sarah Hughes.

Hughes now had a chance — slim, but a chance nonetheless. But she tried not to see it that way.

"I didn't want to skate for a gold medal," she said later. "I went out and had a great time. I said, 'This is the Olympics. I want to do the best.'"

Her love of skating shone through in the minutes that followed. Hughes sailed across the ice with utter grace. She twirled with dizzying speed and jumped with fearless abandon, landing the first-ever triple/triple combination by an Olympian. Through it all, she wore a look of pure joy.

Hughes won the gold with her near-flawless skating routine; she won the hearts of millions for that look — the look of true Olympic spirit.

✶ CHAPTER ELEVEN ✶

2004–2006

Back to Athens and Into the Future

In 2004, the Olympic Games came full circle when they were held in Athens, Greece. It was, as one Greek organizer put it, "a homecoming for world sport and the chance to rediscover ancient virtues."

Two nations, the United States and Iraq, honored one of those virtues. These countries had been at war since 2003, yet both sent representatives to the Games — a nod to the ancient Olympic Truce.

Sadly, however, the promise not to cheat as laid out in the Athletes' Oath was not honored by all. Twenty-four athletes were discovered to have used drugs banned by the IOC, the most ever. In Games past, these cheats would have put a damper on the competition.

That year, however, IOC president Jacques Rogge put a different, more encouraging spin on the situation by noting that "every positive test catches a cheat and protects a clean athlete."

And there were plenty of "clean" and incredibly talented athletes at these Games. One such star was a swimmer from America named Michael Phelps.

Phelps, the son of a schoolteacher and a Maryland State Trooper, had been swimming competitively since he was six years old. He also played lacrosse, soccer, and baseball until he was twelve, when he gave up the fields for the pool. Phelps went to his first Olympics in 2000 at age fifteen, where he came in fifth in the 200-meter butterfly. Now nineteen, he returned to his second Games.

"My goal," he said, "is one Olympic gold medal. Not many people in this world can say, 'I'm an Olympic gold medalist.'"

As it turned out, Phelps had the opportunity to say that very thing *six times*! Only swimmer Mark Spitz won more gold medals in a single Olympics. And Phelps also earned two bronze medals, making him the first American to earn eight medals at one Games.

"You can't put a limit on anything," Phelps once said. "The more you dream, the farther you get."

Many other Olympians reached their dreams in these Games as well. Moroccan runner Hicham El Guerrouj was one of the swiftest men on the planet. Yet at the 1996 Olympics, he came in dead last in the 1,500-meter race when he fell after his knee collided with another runner's heel. Four years later, he was in the lead in the same race only to be overtaken 25 meters from the finish line.

But 2004 would be El Guerrouj's year. First up was the 1,500-meter. He was in the lead for much of the race. But then, with only 40 meters to go, another runner, Bernard Lagat, drew alongside him.

The two ran neck and neck and for the briefest moment it looked like Lagat was ahead. But with his last ounce of energy, El Guerrouj edged into the lead and crossed the finish line mere centimeters before Lagat.

Tears of joy streaked his face as he jogged around the track for his victory lap — and he wasn't finished yet. Spurred on by his first Olympic gold, he raced past the front runner in the 5,000-meter to claim his second. Elated, El Guerrouj fell to his knees and laid his forehead on the track, knowing that only one other runner, the great Paavo Nurmi of the 1924 Olympics, had taken gold in both events.

Two marathon runners would not be as fortunate. In the men's race, Brazilian runner Vanderlei de Lima was in the lead with just seven kilometers to go. Then suddenly, a crazed man rushed into his path and shoved him off the course into a crowd of spectators!

De Lima recovered quickly but later admitted, "When I saw the man who was jumping on me I was scared, because I didn't know what could happen to me, whether he was armed with a knife, a revolver or something and whether he was going to kill me." Then he added, "If you stop in a marathon, you struggle the next three or four kilometers. It's hard to get your rhythm back."

De Lima crossed the finish line in third place to take the bronze. However, in recognition for his sportsmanlike attitude after the incident, he was also awarded the Pierre de Coubertin Medal.

The women's marathon was not interrupted by an

outsider, but it did see the withdrawal of one of the event's hopefuls. Paula Radcliffe of Great Britain was a world record holder; unfortunately, she would not break any records at the 2004 Games. With only a few kilometers left to go, she was forced to the sidelines, overcome by the heat and humidity.

Heat played no part in the next Olympic Games, held in February of 2006 in Torino, Italy. The slopes in the surrounding mountainsides were packed with plenty of snow and the stands with plenty of cheering fans. Many of those fans donned winter parkas, mittens, and scarves to watch the half-pipe snowboarding competition. Among those competing was American Shaun White. At nineteen years old, the shaggy red-haired boarder was a star of the Winter X-Games and holder of several World Championship titles. An Olympic medal seemed all but certain — until he fell in the first heat. If he was going to reach the finals, he'd have to deliver in his next attempt.

Deliver he did, with the best score of the qualifying round. Up next was the final round. White, the lower part of his face covered with his signature red, white, and blue handkerchief, made it look easy. He sliced his way down one wall and up the other, and flew through the air, flipping, twisting, and grabbing as the crowd whistled and hooted. When he was done, he had earned 46.8 points out a possible 50. No other boarder did as well, giving White the gold even before his second run.

Knowing that, White decided to make some changes in his last Olympic outing. "Well, I just started to have some fun," he said later. "I thought, 'This is the Olympics.'" The result was a run that included one of the biggest frontside airs anyone had ever seen in competition.

Shaun White was for many young spectators the new face of sport — a smart-talking, long-haired dude who also happened to be a fantastic, grounded athlete. He once credited his family for keeping him on the ground even when he was in the air, saying, "No matter how cool you think you are or whatever, your family is always there to kinda put you in check. And you really can't trade that for anything. Because no matter what . . . they're still gonna like you, you know what I mean? And I think that's something to hold onto."

Other athletes at the Torino Games captured other aspects of the Olympic spirit. One such athlete was a speed skater named Joey Cheek.

In 1996, the United States Olympic Committee (USOC) began a program of awarding athletes bonuses for medals. Gold medals would earn them $25,000, silver $15,000, and bronze $10,000. It was a controversial program as it seemed to go against the Olympic ideal of amateurism, but in 2006, the program was still in place.

On February 13, Joey Cheek won the gold medal in the 500-meter speed skate. That night at a press conference, he made an announcement that startled many. He was donating his bonus money to a charity named Right to Play that helps suffering children in the war-torn area of Darfur in Sudan. A few nights later, he added a silver medal to his gold — another $15,000 to his charitable donation.

Cheek knew exactly why he wanted to donate the money. "My family, friends, teammates . . . have all invested time, money, and emotion so that I could pursue my dream," he once said. "I wanted to attempt to give a voice to a people who had none. Without the support of others nothing great could ever be accomplished."

✶ EPILOGUE ✶

Beijing and Beyond

When the Summer Olympics open in Beijing in 2008, they will mark the twenty-ninth time these contests have been held since 1896. As in years past, hundreds of thousands of athletes will live out their own Olympic dreams and accomplish great things with the support of those closest to them.

But in truth, the Olympic dream is kept alive when a boy or a girl first falls in love with a sport. New Olympians are born on the slopes and in the rinks, on the mats and in the arenas, on the track and in the pool, every day. Nurturing those hopefuls takes money, time, and energy.

Yet in the end, when that newly crowned champion steps onto the podium amidst the strains of his or her national anthem and the cheers of the crowd, all the hard work and sacrifice seem like distant memories.

For that Olympian — and all those who competed before and will compete in the future — the dream has come true.

Read them all!

*Previously published as Crackerjack Halfback

All available in paperback from Little, Brown and Company

**Previously published as Pressure Play

Matt Christopher®

Muhammad Ali

Lance Armstrong

Kobe Bryant

Jennifer Capriati

Dale Earnhardt Sr.

Jeff Gordon

Ken Griffey Jr.

Mia Hamm

Tony Hawk

Ichiro

Derek Jeter

Randy Johnson

Michael Jordan

Yao Ming

Shaquille O'Neal

Jackie Robinson

Alex Rodriguez

Babe Ruth

Curt Schilling

Sammy Sosa

Tiger Woods

Welcome to the greatest events in sports!

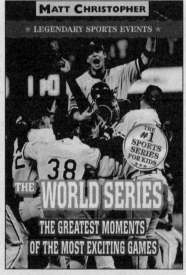